Home Life
In Grandma's Day

by Valerie Weber
and Geneva Lewis

Carolrhoda Books, Inc./Minneapolis

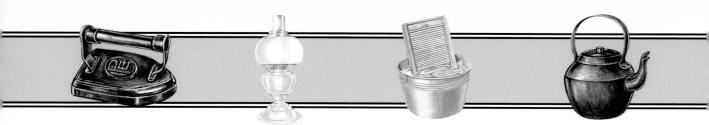

Carolrhoda Books, Inc., A Division of the Lerner Publishing Group
241 First Avenue North, Minneapolis, MN 55401 U.S.A.

Website address: www. lernerbooks.com

Planning and production by Discovery Books
Edited by Faye Gardner
Text designed by Ian Winton
Illustrations by Stuart Lafford
Commissioned photography by Sabine Beaupré and Jim Wend

The publishers would like to thank Geneva Lewis for her help in the preparation of this book.

Library of Congress Cataloging-in-Publication Data

Weber, Valerie.
  Home life in grandma's day / by Valerie Weber and Geneva Lewis ; [illustrations by Stuart Lafford].
      p.   cm. — (In grandma's day)
  Includes index.
  Summary: While focusing on home life, this account presents the story of Geneva Lewis, an African American who grew up in segregated De Quincy, Louisiana, during the 1940s.
   ISBN 1-57505-329-2 (alk. paper)
   1. Afro-Americans—Louisiana—De Quincy—Social life and customs—Juvenile literature. 2. Afro-Americans—Segregation—Louisiana—De Quincy—History—20th century—Juvenile literature. 3. De Quincy (La.)—Social life and customs—Juvenile literature. 4. Lewis, Geneva, 1934–   —Childhood and youth—Juvenile literature. [1. Afro-Americans—Louisiana—De Quincy—Social life and customs. 2. De Quincy (La.)—Social life and customs. 3. Lewis, Geneva, 1934–   —Childhood and youth. 4. Afro-Americans—Biography. 5. Women—Biography.] I. Lewis, Geneva, 1934–   . II. Lafford, Stuart, ill. III. Title. IV. Series: Weber, Valerie. In grandma's day.
F379.D46W43 1999
976.3'54—dc21   98-12286

Printed in Hong Kong
Bound in the United States of America
1 2 3 4 5 6 - OS - 04 03 02 01 00 99

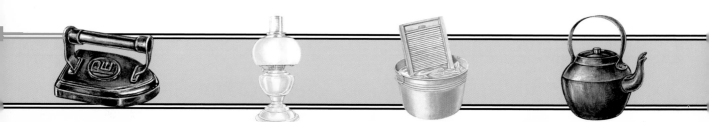

Contents

Home Life in the Deep South

My name is Geneva Lewis. I'm the mother of eight children and the grandmother of eighteen grandchildren. I'm the great-grandmother of four. In this picture, you can see me with three of my grandchildren: Tanisha and Jessica are eleven years old and Stephanie is five years old.

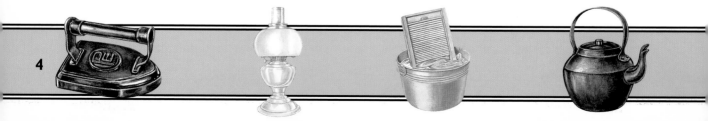

I was born on March 16, 1934, in a small town in Louisiana called De Quincy. The photo on the right was taken when I was eleven years old. I had one older sister named Lucille and two older brothers named Wilbert and Johnny Jr. My dad worked for the Missouri Pacific Railroad in the machine shop, and my mother worked in a laundry and did housework for other families.

My mother is the one on the right in this photo taken at the laundry.

Life in the 1930s and 1940s was different in many ways. Let me tell you about my home and childhood in Louisiana.

My Home Town

When I was growing up in the 1930s and 1940s (and until the early 1960s), African Americans were

called colored people. In Louisiana, and in other states, blacks had to use the back entrance to certain places, travel in separate railroad cars, and attend different churches and schools than white people. This was called segregation.

The school photo below was taken when I was ten. I'm sitting first from the right in the second row.

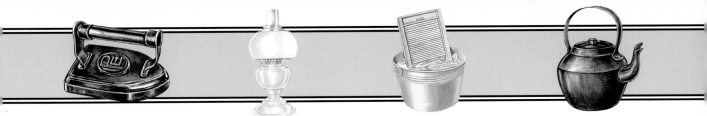

The town of De Quincy was divided by railroad tracks into Uptown, where the white families lived, and the area where the black families lived. Our part of town didn't have a name. The photo below shows how De Quincy's business area looked when I was young.

The people in De Quincy were friendly, and our neighborhood felt very safe. We could leave the house unlocked. Neighbors could come into our house when we were gone to borrow a cup of flour or sugar. Friends came to my door almost every day, asking me to play.

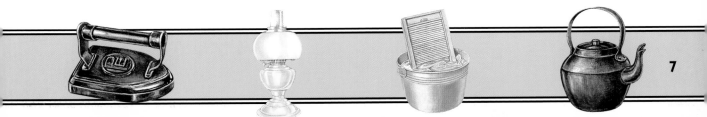

My Cozy Home

The photograph below shows the house I grew up in. I was already an adult when the photo was taken. It shows me sitting in the front yard with my mom and baby son.

Our house had three bed-rooms, a living room, a dining room, and a kitchen. They were all nice-sized rooms. My sister and I had our own room, too, but we shared a bed.

The boys had their own room. We didn't have electricity, but oil lamps gave our house a warm glow at night.

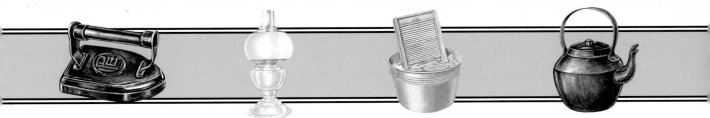

Our home was heated by a black iron heater in the dining room. My dad and brothers cut the wood that we all fed into it. Since none of the other rooms had a heater, the dining room was the only warm room in the winter. Fortunately, Louisiana is in the southern United States, and the temperature rarely gets below forty degrees there.

Like most people in our neighborhood, we didn't have an indoor flush toilet when I was growing up. Throughout the 1940s, we had an outhouse, a tiny building with a hole in the ground and a seat above the hole. Unlike some families, who used catalogs cut into squares, we had regular, store-bought toilet paper. We dumped lye down the toilet to keep it smelling clean.

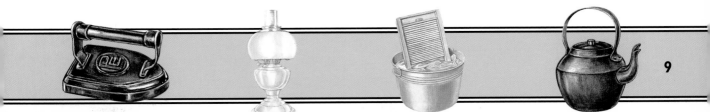

Iceboxes and Tin Tubs

Like many families in our neighborhood, we didn't have a refrigerator. Instead, we used a wooden cabinet called an icebox. The ice inside the icebox kept our food cold. It melted into a drip pan beneath the icebox.

Sometimes the iceman came in his truck to deliver ice in big blocks of twenty-five or fifty pounds to put in the icebox. At other times, my dad would go to the ice-house in town and buy a big block of ice. He would wrap a thick piece of twine around the ice for a handle and carry it home.

Instead of the gas or electric stove that your family has, we had a wood-burning cast-iron stove in the kitchen. We used the stove to cook our food and warm water.

Since we didn't have a bathroom, we took our baths in the kitchen. My mom would heat a big pot of water on the stove and dump it into a big tin tub. That's where we all took turns bathing two or three times a week. I was happy I didn't have to share my bath with anyone. My friends in bigger families had to take baths two kids at a time.

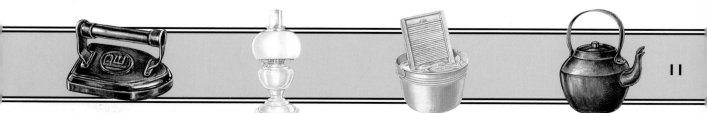

Homemade Clothes

At the beginning of each school year, my mom bought us three or four outfits, a pair of shoes for school, and a pair of shoes for church. That was it for the year!

In the early 1940s, the United States fought in World War II. Our soldiers needed clothes, food, and weapons. With posters like the one on the right, our government urged families to reuse things. We tried to make our clothes, our food, and even our cars last longer so that soldiers could have all they needed. If we did rip something or wear out a spot, my mother mended it right away.

USE IT UP – WEAR IT OUT – MAKE IT DO!

OUR LABOR AND OUR GOODS ARE FIGHTING

I was a chubby child. Because it was hard to find clothes that fit me, my mother paid a seamstress in the neighborhood to make my clothes. She sewed my dresses on a beautiful black-and-gold sewing machine.

The machine sat on a wooden desk and had little drawers underneath to hold spools of thread, spare needles, and other sewing equipment. Under the desk was a treadle that the seamstress rocked back and forth with her feet to power the machine. The faster she rocked, the faster the machine sewed.

In this photo, you can see my friend Nora Mae in a cotton dress similar to the ones I wore.

After School

After school, I came straight home and changed my clothes to keep them clean so I could wear them again. Then I did my homework, lots of it, at the kitchen table. If I had any problems, my sister helped me with them.

We also worked together on household chores. It was my sister's job to make supper and mine to do the dishes. It seemed like my brothers got off easy. All they had to do was chop wood for the heater and the stove.

After my parents got home from work, around five-thirty, we ate a light supper such as fried salt pork and sweet potatoes or sandwiches. We almost always drank milk, although some-

times my mother would buy us soda as a treat. Sometimes I would go to the store for a candy bar after supper. Snickers were my favorite!

After supper, my family often listened to the little wooden radio that sat on the dining room table. I liked mystery shows like *The Squeaking Door* and *Inner Sanctum*.

Cleaning the House

While we did some housework every week-day after school, Saturday was the main day for doing chores. Every Saturday after breakfast, I helped clean the house with my sister. My mom

was usu-ally cleaning another family's house. Dad worked some Saturdays. On others, he was either home with us or out fishing. In the picture on the left, you can see what I looked like when I was twelve years old.

It was my job to wash and wax all the floors in the house. I used a mop to wash the floor but got down on my hands and knees with a rag to wax the floor with Johnson's Liquid Wax. It was a hard job, but I liked the way the floor shone afterward.

My sister had to dust the furniture, using a rag to wipe down all the wooden tables and straight-backed wooden chairs in the living room and dining room. Our couch had curved wooden arms with designs carved into them that were hard to dust. If it took my sister longer to do her jobs than it did for me to do mine, I helped her by starting the laundry.

Doing the Laundry

Like most of our neighbors, we didn't have an electric washing machine, and no one had the kind of electric or gas dryer your family might have.

As you can see from the picture on the right, electric washing machines looked different in those days. Instead of spinning clothes dry, this machine used an attachment called a wringer to individually wring out each item of clothing.

Doing the laundry by hand was a big job that took most of the day. We heated a tub of water over a fire in our backyard. We washed our laundry on a washboard, using a long pole to swish it through the soapy water. Then we rinsed the laundry in a big tub and wrung it out by hand.

Finally, we used wooden clothespins to hang the laundry on a line in the backyard. The clothes always smelled fresh when we were done. We didn't have an electric iron then, so we heated a metal iron on top of the stove to press our clothes.

Mom's Home Cooking

My mom used to raise chickens for our family. Most of the time, they ran around freely in the backyard. When it was time to eat one, she would catch a hen and put it in a coop for a day or two so that it couldn't eat. That made the inside of the chicken easier to clean. Then she wrung its neck and dumped the chicken into a pot of boiling water to loosen its feathers. Finally, she put the chicken in a dishpan and plucked its feathers.

Sometimes, those chickens were roasted to make our big midday meal. My mom was a wonderful cook, and even during hard times, we ate very well. I loved her pork chops with mustard and cabbage greens. My whole family liked her "potato pond," which was really a kind of bread. We devoured it without butter, hot out of the oven.

For dessert, we always had cake or some other treat. My favorites were yellow cake with chocolate frosting and home-cooked banana or bread pudding.

Fun with Friends and Family

In the 1930s and 1940s, there were no electronic games, computers, televisions, or VCRs. Like many families then, we had few toys and made up our own games. We liked to play house in the field behind our street. We used old tin tubs for furniture and pretended that leaves and twigs were food and old cans were cooking pots and pans.

After the noon meal, if my sister and I had finished with our chores, we swung on the wood-en swing that hung from a tree in our back-yard. I also played with children in the neighbor-hood a lot. My best friend was Agnes Mays.

I had two rag dolls, Martha and Edna, that were made by my mom out of old stockings. Black dolls were nearly impossible to find in those days; the stores only sold white dolls.

I also had a game called Marble Mosaics, which I shared with my sister. We spent hours arranging the colored marbles into different shapes and patterns.

Sitting on the Front Porch

Summers in Louisiana were very hot—often over one hundred degrees! Few houses had air conditioning, either. Like most families in our neighborhood, my family spent a lot of time out on the front porch, where it was a little cooler than in the house.

In the evening, neighbors would stop by to chat with us. Television was very new then, and few people owned a set. We didn't have a phone, and neither did any of our neighbors.

Visiting with our neighbors was a great source of information and fun. Sometimes my father brought out his violin, and our next-door neighbor came over with his accordion. The other kids and I made up dances in the front yard to their lively music.

On hot nights, it was a big treat to make lemonade. We squeezed fresh lemons into a pitcher, added sugar and

water, and stirred. To make it really cold, my dad chipped ice off the big block in the icebox and dropped it into each of our glasses. It was so refreshing to suck on the ice chips after I gulped down my lemonade.

My Sunday Best

On Sundays, we went to the Evergreen Baptist Church, which you can see in the picture below. I always wore my best dress. It was a little fancier than my schoolday dresses, and sometimes it had a bow or two. This photo shows me in my best Sunday clothes. I was fifteen years old and felt very grown-up.

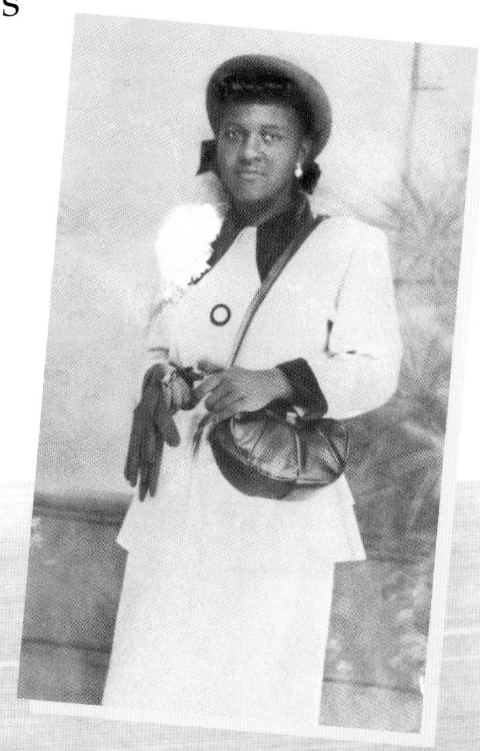

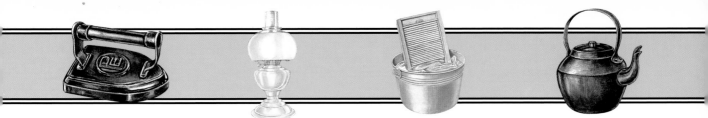

We had to be at Sunday school at nine o'clock in the morning, and regular services started at eleven o'clock. The photo below shows some of the children and teachers who attended Sunday school.

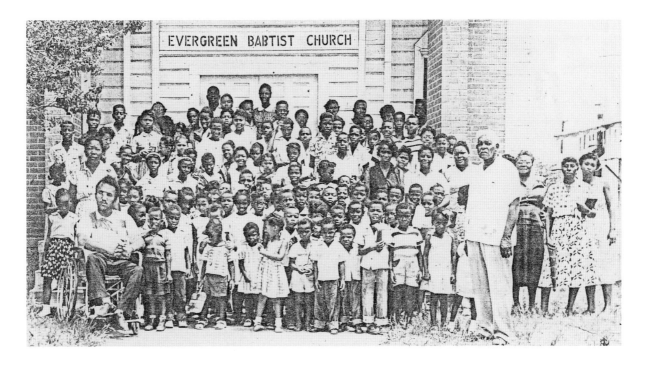

My sister was in the children's choir. The sound of their beautiful voices floated over us, inspiring our worship. After church, we would come home to one of my mom's great meals.

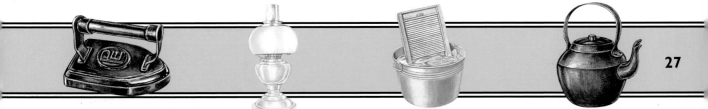

The Picture Show

Sometimes after church — if we had finished our homework — we could go to the picture show, which is what the movies were called in my day.

We were not allowed to mix with white customers, so we went into the theater through a separate entrance and sat upstairs in the balcony. The white families sat below us on the main floor.

I liked the cartoons and cowboy movies a lot. My favorite cowboy shows starred Gene Autry or Roy Rogers and Dale Evans. During intermission, which was the time between the cartoons and the main movie, a man came around to our seats, selling candy, popcorn, and soda.

When I grew up, I moved to a busy big city in the northern United States. But I often look back on those days in a small southern town and wonder what it would be like to live there still.

Glossary

greens: leafy plants cooked as vegetables

icebox: a cabinet that keeps food cool with a large block of ice

intermission: a break between parts of a show

lye: a strong cleaning solution made from wood ashes

picture show: a movie shown in a theater

salt pork: fatty pork preserved with salt

seamstress: a woman who sews for a living

segregation: the setting apart of one racial group from another racial group

washboard: a rectangular board with a rippled surface used for scrubbing clothes

wringer: a device that presses water out of clothes

For Further Reading

Doney, Meryl. *Games*. New York: Franklin Watts, 1996.

Duden, Jane. *Timeline: 1940s*. New York: Crestwood House, 1989.

Rubel, David. *The United States in the 20th Century*. New York: Scholastic, 1995.

Stein, R. Conrad. *The Home Front*. Chicago: Children's Press, 1986.

Trotter, Joe William, Jr. *From a Raw Deal to a New Deal?: African Americans, 1929-1945*. New York: Oxford University Press, 1996.

Whitman, Sylvia. *V Is for Victory: The American Home Front during World War II*. Minneapolis, Minn.: Lerner Publications Co.,1993.

Index